THIS BOOK BELONGS TO

....

....

Made in the USA
Columbia, SC
23 May 2022

60816661R00055